LOSING SEASON

LOSING
SEASON

Jack Ridl

CavanKerry ◈ Press LTD.

Library of Congress Cataloging-in-Publication Data
Ridl, Jack.
Losing season / Jack Ridl.
p. cm.
ISBN-13: 978-1-933880-15-0
ISBN-10: 1-933880-15-5
1. Sports–Poetry. I. Title.

PS3568.I3593L67 2009
811'.54–dc22

2009022607

Cover art, Federico Jordhan © 2009
Author photograph by Louis Schakel
Cover and book design by Peter Cusack

First Edition 2009
Printed in the United States of America

CavanKerry Press Ltd.
Fort Lee, New Jersey
www.cavankerrypress.org

CavanKerry Press is proud to publish the works
of established poets of merit and distinction.

CavanKerry Press is grateful for the
support it receives from the
New Jersey State Council on the Arts.

OTHER BOOKS BY JACK RIDL

The Same Ghost (Poetry)
Between (Poetry)
Poems from The Same Ghost and Between
After School (Chapbook)
Against Elegies (Chapbook)
Broken Symmetry (Poetry)
Outside the Center Ring (Chapbook)
Approaching Poetry with Peter Schakel (Textbook)
Approaching Literature with Peter Schakel (Textbook)

All you learn from losing's how to lose.
—Coach

CONTENTS

THE FOURTH QUARTER

LOSING SEASON

Losing Season: Everybody Talks

It's the way December
turns to March. It's
the teeth on the right side
tight, all eyes finding a way
to see around the corner. It's

not making the coffee,
not saying good morning
anymore, not fixing
the dent in your car,
the draft under the door,
the difference between
the two of you.

THE FIRST QUARTER

At Fifty

Coach hurls the ball against the garage door,
grabs it on the rebound. He's missed ten
in a row. He steps to the line, bounces
the ball twice, hard, and the fans from
thirty years ago send their hopes across
their weary lungs. He listens to the hush
of the home crowd while the taunts
of those from out of town float through
the rafters down across the backboard,
spinning around and around the rim.
He slams the ball one more time, feels
the leather, eyes the hoop, shoots.
The ball caroms off the back of the rim, rolls
across the driveway into the herb garden
his wife planted the year they found this house.
Once he could drop nine out of ten
from the line, hit half his jump shots
from twenty feet. Coach sits down at
the top of the key, stares, sees himself
bringing it up against the press, faking,
shaking his shoulders, stutter stepping, shifting
the ball left hand to right, then back, then up,
his legs exploding, his wrist firing, the ball
looping up, down, through the hoop, making
the net shimmer, the crowd roar. He gets up,
goes over to the garden, reaches for the ball,
stops and pulls some weeds growing through
the oregano, basil, sage, and thyme.

First Cut

The night before,
eight of the players
slept. Each of the rest
lay wondering if his name
would not be on the list.
"Tomorrow we'll post
first cuts," Coach had said.
"If you're not on the list,
you're still on the team.
If your name is there . . ."
He shrugged. Twenty-two
would go to look, hoping
to find themselves among
the chosen. For years
their names were only
something they had
answered to. But now,
hurled back to the earth's
first days, they could feel
the finger of the caller
of names point. God said,
"Smith," and Smith
walked on among the
elect. On the wall, next
to Coach's office door,
the list. Some came
early, stood, stared,
and left. Some waited.
Coach had told them
not to say a word.
Some held out past lunch,

then gave in, went,
and saw. That night,
Coach called the chosen
together at center court.
"All right," he said, "you
made it this far. There
will be one more cut.
Twelve of you will make it.
We'll go one more week. Now,
wind sprints." The others
went to look for something
else to do, wished
they'd never tried, felt a fire
burning around their names.

Coach Goes Down the Hall
Wondering Where All the Men Went

"Where are they, for Christ's sake?"
Coach wonders as he passes
what used to pass for men
slouched against the row of lockers,
gazing. What the hell do they think?
He feels he wants to punch one,
ram him up against a locker,
jam him inside, slam the door, spin
the lock to a code impossible to crack.
His short hair burns. His years of bending
over math and dribbling with his left hand
turn to stone. They stand around and plan
to escape the very things he dreamed of.
What went wrong? Dribbling mattered.
So did math. So did all the nights spent
cramming for the credits he would need
to hold his job, his place in class and
on the bench. But them? He shakes
his head, sucks in his gut, and feels
the awful smirk behind him, feels
the urge to throw an elbow, trip
any of them driving for the hoop.

Coach's Daughter

She stares at her cornflakes.
"What's the matter?" Coach
asks, honestly. She raises
her eyes. "What is it?" She
wants to say, "Nothing."
Everyone says, "Nothing."
Her lips tighten. He thinks
she is beautiful. He is afraid
of her, her soft hair, her long
fingers, her eye shadow.
He tries not to think about
the country between them.
He wants to hear her say,
"It's OK here. And you
are welcome here." But
this country goes on
for as long as you can walk.
There are no borders.
Coach knows he needs borders.

Assistant Coach Thinks about Taking Over

Before heading to the game,
he glances back over his
shoulder into the mirror
at the bald spot, size
of a silver dollar centered
on the back of his head.
"It's time," he thinks
again. "They want to run."
He hit for eighteen a game,
still plays summer ball, can
cut down the lane, elbow
his way in. This is his seventh
year sitting, yelling nothing
more than "C'mon, hit
the boards, stick to your man."
During a game, he waits
for Coach to ask him
what he thinks. During
practice, he stands along
the sideline, talks to the guys
about how things are going,
wonders if they think
he could do a better job.

Opening Game: Halftime

Coach is pissed.
"Seventeen. How the hell
did you let them get ahead
by seventeen!" They hang
their heads like bad dogs.
Scrub can only think of
Jennie, her long brown
hair, her sweatered breasts.
Coach breaks a piece of chalk
and diagrams some dream
to bring them back. They
know better. "Now get out
there, and for God's sake,
don't make us look any worse."

Scrub Dreams of Taking the Last Shot

Thirty-one seconds on the clock. Coach is down on one knee, screaming at Tommy to get the ball across mid-court and call time-out. We're down by one. Time-out. In the huddle, Coach slaps Frank behind the head. "Look at this. Look. Now, you, Frank, you get the ball to Jimmy. Frank, you hear me? OK. Now, get the ball to Jimmy. Then, Frank, you break down the lane like you're gonna get it back. Got it? OK. Then, Jimmy, you look for Scrub who'll be breaking out to the line after Frank goes by. Frank, you're gonna screen Scrub's man. OK? Now, it's just the same as in practice. No different. No different. Just the same. Just the . . ." And all Scrub can hear is this roar, this sense that the roof is opening and a train is tumbling slowly across the sky. He looks over at Jennie. She's shoving her fist toward the scoreboard and yelling, "Come on Blue! Come on Blue!" The horn sounds. They all reach in, grab Coach's hand. "OK. OK. OK. OK. OK. OK." Frank tosses it in to Jimmy. 28, 27, 26, 25. Jimmy dribbles left, back right; his man presses close; Jimmy keeps the ball tight to his right side, keeps his left arm out. He holds his head high, at an angle. 18, 17, 16, 15. He passes to Tommy. Tommy looks inside, fakes a pass, head fakes, tosses back to Jimmy. The train is rolling, the crowd, the clock, Jennie is shrieking, "C'mon, c'mon, c'mon!" 12, 11, 10. Jimmy's still dribbling. Coach is back down on his knee, clapping. "OK. OK. OK." Frank cuts down the lane. Scrub fakes left, then starts for the line; Jimmy looks to his right, catches Scrub open; Scrub turns, fires . . . The last dance, "Good-night, sweetheart, well, it's time to go. Good-night sweetheart, good-night." And Jennie cups her hand around Scrub's neck.

Shower

The scum on the shower walls
and floor makes Coach think,
"Stuff grows no matter what."
He slides his toe across the
smooth green surface of it all.
Surrounded by his players'
dirty jokes he feels the spray
mean against his face, turns it
even hotter, tries to open
every pore, let out each woman
he remembers. Next to him,
Star works a lather into his thick
hair, leans back and smiles,
the water splashing off his
shoulders. Coach wipes his face,
looks at his skin that twists
and folds like some damned
lizard's. He laughs and lets
the water fall across his back,
looks down, sees his feet and
feels like some strange creature
from some swamp that stood up
in the rain and walked. He waits
until the players empty out,
hears them snapping towels,
banging lockers. He waits until
their last laugh drifts away, turns
off his shower, shivers
when he dries between his toes.

Trainer Teaches Eight
Phys Ed Classes a Day

And he goes to
every game. He
knows pain's
every name, lets it
lead him through
its landscape
to the perfect
touch, the perfect
place to stay.

He's a priest
listening
to the mortal
sins within
the skin, the
muscles, blood,
and bone.

If pain refuses
to confess,
he prays
his prayer,
says, "Can you
still go?"
Knows.

Manager

At home, in his room, after practice,
manager dreams of coming off the bench,
seven seconds left, behind by one, and
firing in a jump shot at the buzzer.
His teammates carry him off the floor.
The fans roar long after the lights on
the scoreboard go out. At the dance, he
turns down every wink and smile, stands
against the cafeteria wall, even the toughs,
in tight jeans nodding his way before
their anemic girls pull them out to their
cars, engines running in the parking lot.
He lies back. The dream floats off
on its own. He looks at his letter jacket,
at the *W*, wishes he could answer "Guard."

Coach Losing His Daughter

She stares at his players
who turn him into aging wood,
make him sexless as his little finger.
When he tries to talk to her,
his sentences dissolve, the nouns
and verbs all floating mute
into the sky's blue ear.
He knows why his players
lift and curl. He sees them
tightening their belts. Bodies
that well built should build
a house, knock a bully
on his can. But after practice,
Coach can only see his daughter
getting in their cars, feel
their muscles sweating on her skin.

Jim Kenner Owned a Variety Store

Keeping the place open till five
was often more than Jim could stand.
He'd owned it now for thirty years.
When he was a kid, he'd dreamed
of staying here in his hometown
and opening a store. This one sold
everything: ribbons, place mats,
stationery, caps, toys, games, pens,
pencils, paper clips, you name it.
If under ten bucks, Jim had it.
His radio played "Beautiful Music,"
and his voice was always friendly
asking Coach how he was doing. He
loved the games: came early, sat in
the same seat, screamed, "Deeeee-
fense," slapped each player on
the shoulder when he walked by
the bench to take a leak and get
a Coke. One day he told Coach,
"The doctor says I have to take
it easy. How in hell do I do that?
I hate busted plays, bad calls, and
after every game we lose, I swear
I'll sell the store, never see another
game, move to Florida, just quit."

Pep Rally

The gym is draped
in banners. "Kill
the Lions," "Maul
the Lions," "Turn the
Lions into Pussycats."
The players stand
solemn as pallbearers.
The cheerleaders keep
the crowd screaming,
"Let's go Comets!"
Coach steps to the mike,
signals everyone into
silence. The cheerleaders
sit cross-legged, stare
at the team, feel
their own smoothed legs.
"We're ready," Coach
assures the crowd. "Are
you?" "Yeah!" "Are you?"
"Yeah!" "Let me hear it!"
"Yeah! Yeah! Yeah!"
The cheerleaders stand,
smooth their skirts.
The students stand.
The band plays "Fight,
Fight, Comets." The players
raise their fists. Coach
yells, "We wanna hear that
at the game tonight!" and rams
his elbow in doubt's gut.

Band Director

After looking over the list
of fight songs for the game,
Band Director remembers
playing trombone in this same
room. He practiced two hours
every day. While other guys
worked on their cars, played
ball, picked up girls, hung out,
he'd be sliding the long arm
of his horn, hoping the notes
would get him out. He got
good enough to go to college,
major in music, play jazz in
bars until he graduated. Later
he got himself an Ed. degree.
Tonight he'll hear the notes hit,
missed, all hanging in the gym's
dissonant air. He'll glance over
his shoulder as the team warms
up, turn back, give his band
the downbeat, direct them
while he stares above the crowd.

Pacing Before the Game

Like zoo lions
on a hot afternoon,
the players walk
back and forth
in front of
their lockers.
No one says
a word. They
stare through
the floor into
the center of the earth
where all losers
end up, far
from the light of God,
day, or a back room.
Lips drawn, fists
clenched around
their sweaty palms,
they feel the long season
tighten in their legs,
the practices float
up and into their
shoulders. They
each feel a sneaky
laugh rising in
the back of their
brain. Suddenly
they want to leap
into the stands,
grab some kid who
gets *As* in math

and put him up against
the other team. But
there's only the clock,
the door, the gym
at the end of the hall.

Before the Game

"A lot of slush tonight,"
Custodian thinks, looking
over at the row of mops
leaning against the wall
of the boiler room. "I
clean up after everyone."

The crowd is coming in,
stomping the snow
off their boots, shaking
the flakes from their coats.
He grabs a bucket, takes
a mop, puts them by the door.

He thinks of his son, a teacher
sixty miles away, who'd played
guard, averaged fourteen and
six assists his senior year. He'd
let him in the gym on Sundays.
They'd gone one-on-one.
He'd won a game or two.

He remembers going
out with Cindy Cross.
She married a car dealer.
His hands feel like young birds.

The team comes bursting
through the locker room
door, clapping, yelling past
him. He slaps each player
on the shoulder, says,
"Good luck. Go get 'em."

He Sits on the End of the Bench

—for Don Johnson

He's sat there every game
since Coach took over. He
lives at home with his father.
Sometimes someone gives
him a job to do: clean out
the pavilion in the park,
rake some leaves, shovel
some snow. When Coach
told him he could sit by
the last player, the kid
grabbed Coach, holding
on until Coach pulled
him off and, shrugging,
patted him on the back.
He's been on the bench
ever since. After the team
warms up, he sacks the
balls in a gray canvas bag.
During time-outs he stands
just outside the huddle.
When a player gets off
the bench or comes out,
he slaps him on the back.
One time, after a loss,
some toughs beat him up
in the parking lot. Coach
took him home. He wears
his letter jacket everywhere.

Ref Comes in from Out of Town

Heading for the game, Ref
sits behind the wheel, radio
tuned to a Big Band station.
Each job sets him on the road
staring through the high beams
into another winter storm.

"I'm the ref," he tells
the parking lot attendant.
"They reserve a spot."
He avoids everyone's eyes.
In his dressing room, he runs
over a few rules with
his partner, drinks a Coke,
pulls on the gray pants,
black shoes, black-and-white
striped knit shirt, drapes
the whistle around his neck.
He knows his stuff but also
feels a whisper rising up
his neck. "You blow a call . . ."

Driving home, sixty bucks
in his wallet, he listens
to the news, hears the
score of the game,
feels a shiver of relief
for the twenty-point spread,
tries to shake out the mistakes,
to picture his wife asleep

in the warm bed, his arms
around her, her taking him,
making the game easy,
the outcome one he's sure of.

Closing the Gym

Equipment Man wonders for a second
if he's forgotten anything: the dryers

are off, the uniforms are stacked,
the shoes are out to air. He put

out his pipe, cleaned the blackboard,
fixed the zipper in Watts's warm-up,

turned off the radio, turned off
the lights, locked the door. A stiff wind

blows across the parking lot. He
sees a car, its motor running, the exhaust

a cloud floating almost frozen. He walks
to his car, scrapes the windshield, thinking

of his wife and how in high school
here, after a game, they'd fumble

under each other's woolen coats,
not knowing that their hands

were learning how to hold them
through a life filled with repairs.

THE SECOND QUARTER

Bad Night at Practice

Star wants to walk off,
hang it up, head
home and lie down,
watch TV, join
the crowd and
fall in love
with Betty,
Carol, Jane,
Norine, and Deb.
He's sick
of Coach's voice,
hears it
in the halls,
in class, in
bed, on any date.
He's tired
of his own right hand,
how it feels alone
without a ball, tired
of white socks,
neat shirts, firm
handshakes, hope.
He wants to quit,
hurl the game ball
through a window,
follow it anywhere it goes.

The Principal Assigned Him to Sell Tickets

Tonight he's anywhere but here: the
opera, movies, circus, Ferris wheel,
the theater, the symphony. "Two dollars.
Two dollars. Fifty cents. Two dollars.
Fifty cents." He never looks up, takes
the money, slides the ticket to the buyer,
wonders who it is: parent, fan, some
lonely man or woman looking for a crowd.
When he closes the window, he glances
at the scoreboard, then leaves. At home,
he tunes in the game on his radio, brews
some coffee, checks over the math problems
handed in that afternoon. The numbers float
like music in his head. He loves the
harmonies of algebra, geometry. They come
from some deep hole in space, join behind
his forehead and create a heaven: certain,
wordless, balanced, silent. Each play,
he thinks, could be an equation, each
pass leading to each pass, working
like a theorem, leading to a basket. The game
could be as musical as math. He hears
the play-by-play man yell, "Coach
has slammed his clipboard down on
the floor!" He looks back to the problems.
When he sees the numbers do not come
together he corrects each error then goes on.

At Harry's Coffee Shop

Dan Perkins says, "They
would've won if Coach
had taken out Frank. He
was three for fifteen. What
the hell was he thinking?
He'd suddenly catch fire?"
Kenny Antonelli's sure
a zone would have forced
them out. "They killed us
underneath." Harry shakes
his head. "Use a press. He
never uses a press. Not
once all year." Tom Smith
rolls his eyes. "You guys
are as dumb as he is. He
shouldn't have cut Ted's
kid. That kid can hit."
The steam from their coffee
clings to the air. Outside,
the snow keeps coming down.

Coach knows exactly what
they're saying. Sometimes
he sees himself standing
behind the counter, wiping
it clean as they come in,
saying, "Coffee, boys?"
asking after their families,
how their own work's going.
He pours the coffees, tosses
them packets of sugar, hands

them the cream, says he's
heard they have the answers.
He then invites them all
to sit beside him on the bench,
tell him what to do, and when.

The End Is Near

"Put in Jesus," he keeps
telling Coach. "He'd win
it for you. He has terrific
hands, great jump shot,
can outleap anyone.
You have a devil in
you, Coach. Satan's
stealing all your plays."
He glares into Coach's
eyes, crawls beneath
his skin, sets little fires
in his nerves. "Coach,
you haven't got much time.
Jesus hates it on the bench."

Stats

Halfway up the bleachers, next
to the cinder block wall, she sits
with her score sheets and freshly
sharpened pencils. She skips
dinner to make sure she gets her
lucky seat, buys a couple hot dogs,
bag of popcorn, cup of Diet Coke.
During the day, her words are never
right; she keeps them clogged
between her knees and neck.
Sometimes she can feel a noun
break free and wander in her brain.
But the adjectives are worst of all,
anarchic, full of terrifying ambushes,
threats to all the silences she's built,
one avoided conversation at a time.
What words are hers she keeps
along her tongue, lets them out
in sleep: yes, home, dance, sky.
After the game, she adds the players'
shots attempted, made, assists, lost
balls, and rebounds, files them in a
dresser drawer beneath her socks.

Outside Kmart

The Salvation Army volunteer
rings her bell, the sound taking
its place with the snowflakes
falling around her. Star,
heading in to pick up a record,
feels trapped between desire
and the bell, feels he's going
to blow a layup, that God
is watching to see if he'll take
the shot or pass to his teammate
cutting down the lane. Inside,
he sees the glow of fluorescence
hovering over the aisles. The bell
continues its single note. Her stare
moves out across the lot between
the cars, between the snowflakes.
Star feels everything in his life
change, the way two faces
suddenly become a vase. All
he wanted was a record, to take
it home, lie back on his bed and
let it let him dream. But now
each person in the store is staring.
Every dollar is a story. Each car
is rusting back to earth. He's
terrified the change he tosses
in the bucket matters, that
the bell's one note will never stop.

Over Christmas Break, Coach Dreams He Visits the Basketball Hall of Fame

Standing out front,
Coach stares at this
final resting place for
winners. The door
slowly opens and
a hand waves him
in, a voice says,
"Stand here among
the best." Coach
wonders if there
is a hall of losers,
a shrine to sleepless
nights, a mausoleum
filled with photographs
of clumsy dribblers,
lead foot centers, low
percentage shooters,
a room where
uniforms hang
from the rafters
like inept ghosts.
On one wall,
under a bright
light, a photo
of his Comets,
last place peering
from their faces.

Lunch Hour

"If I was trying to find
the cure for cancer,"
Coach growls and crumples
up another play, tosses it
toward the wastebasket
in the teacher's lounge where
there's room for every bitch
and moan. Here he dreams
of playing everyone. At each
dead ball, he'd substitute or
call time-out to have a chat.
He'd set up every player for
a hook from forty feet, tell
them all to dribble through
their legs, bounce the ball
off their heads, or spin it
on their middle finger.
They could hurl it high
into the stands, or stop,
hand it to the other team, and
with a sweeping bow, allow
them layup after easy layup.

The Former Great at the Game

Up in the stands, Charlie Carson
sits quietly watching. Before
the game, Coach told the team,
"Know who's here tonight?
Charlie Carson. Charlie Carson,
the best we ever had. All-League
three years in a row. All-American
in college. He's in the stands. And
he'll be watching you." Charlie
watched and saw himself take
a pass from Donny Watts, dribble
down the side then cut across
the lane, stop, fire, hit. He watched
Ken Duncan crash the boards, fling
a long pass out to him; he flips
the ball behind his back to Dewey
Smith for one more easy two.
At halftime, fans stop, say, "Not
like when you and Dewey and . . ."
Charlie smiles. "It's a different
game." He shrugs. After the game,
he goes to the locker room, shakes
each player's hand, wishes them luck.

No Game Plan

The car is jammed between two old oaks,
their branches cutting the negative space
for the moon's slow light sliding itself
across the driver's face, his body
slumped over the wheel. Coach watches
as they try to pry him out. The boy's
mother, still in her nightgown, stands
beside the fire truck. Someone he doesn't
know is holding her hand. The boy's father
suddenly glances at Coach, then turns back
to the Sheriff. Red and blue lights flash,
become a strobe across the night between
the huge white flakes falling over them all.
Coach hears the traffic behind him, feels
the way the wheels sing against the highway.
He wonders why this winter night feels warm,
senses the starlight trailing the snow,
looks up to see the moon fold away
behind the clouds. He reaches in across
his steering wheel to turn his car's lights out
and feels the thought he always dreads. He beats
it back with every other jeer and second guess.

Timer

Time is his to keep.
He watches the seconds
pass, the numbers
blinking back to nothing.
He knows a second more
or less can change a game,
the final score, Coach's
world, a player's night,
the whole town's mood.
He wonders what it
would be like to stop
the clock at the wrong
time, send the game into
an endless chaos, create
an everlasting argument,
excuse. During a close
game, he always feels
a whisper down his finger.

Vendor Sits, Waits for the Halftime Rush

He's surrounded by
Mars Bars, Hershey bars,
Dots, Juicy Fruit gum,
Raisinettes, Beemans,
M&M's, Tootsie Rolls,
red-and-white boxes
of salt-coated popcorn.
Behind him sit
the huge containers
of Coke, 7UP,
Orange Crush—the tubes
twisting out of their
gray fronts, nozzles
pointing at his back.
In front of him,
the pans of hotdogs,
the trays of buns. He
makes change fast,
hears, "All right,
who's next" deep
in his sleep, walks
around all day,
a roll of quarters
spinning in his brain.

Head Cheerleader

At halftime, she finds
an open mirror, checks
her makeup, sweat
glistening on her forehead.
She runs her tongue
along her upper lip, pulls
a comb through her long
brown hair, pushes it up
on the sides, adds a new
line of lipstick, smoothes
down her skirt. On the
way out, she turns and
looks over her shoulder.

Ex-Cheerleader

She remembers
when her days
were filled with fears
of splitting her tights
when she leaped
in front of the fans,
leading them on.

She can feel
an arm around
her waist, the smell
of young sweat,
can see her open
locker, hear the
sound of "See ya
after the game."

She loved to pull
her sweater on over
her head, look
over her shoulder
at her own body
firm in the mirror.

She would spin,
her skirt flouncing,
her head back, her
hair dangling
toward the floor.
She'd laugh long,
loud, shake her

shoulders, then
lean forward, her
hair falling free
across her face.

In the Last Seconds

Coach tries to press another loss
into the back court of his brain.
The players feel their blood quiet,
return to its common wander.
The fans, shaking their heads
like tired dogs, put on their coats,
hats, gloves, leave the bleachers,
go back to what's always there.
The cops shrug, step outside.
Vendor starts counting the till.
In the snow, the parking lot attendants
pierce the darkness with their flashlights.
Coach's wife looks at her hands.
Coach's daughter stares into the rafters,
listens to the words, pretends
they are dead leaves caught in the air.
Manager sacks the towels. Assistant
thinks of being the head coach.
Custodian waits at the locker room door.

The Gym, January

Ice hangs from the roof.
Inside, the great furnace
huffs the heat up into
the bleachers. The cement
hallways shine. The glass
in the trophy case shines.
The trophies shine. In
the locker room, each scarred
locker stands solid against
the concrete block walls,
the benches steady in front.
Against one wall, the blackboard,
chalk and an oily rag sitting
in its trough. In the corner,
a water fountain. One door
opens outside, another
to the court. The gym floor
glistens. The blue *W* in the center
circle glistens. Above it all,
the scoreboard. Outside,
the temperature stays below zero.

THE THIRD QUARTER

Halfway Through

The conversation has moved
back into its common language:
dinner, bills, TV, who died or
moved away, who decided
once again to stay. Two and nine.
Everyone thought they'd be
nine and two. "Maybe if we
hit the boards better, maybe
if we use a press, maybe if
we hit five or six more
field goals every half."
It's January. Grades are due.
Christmas has to be paid for.
Coach's wife thinks about
spending her whole life here.
Coach's daughter dreams of
college in another state.
It's a way to pay the bills.
It's no way to pay the bills.
Again tonight, practice.

Winter Weekend

There's no such thing
as the easy life,
but
you can wear your sorrows
like an old sweater,
as you fill the woodstove,
bank it hot against
a January rain.

Coach knew this.
That's why he
pulled out his letter
sweater, the one
with the gold block *W*
and wore it all weekend,
baked bread, read
the Sunday paper, planned
the next week's practices.
Instead of thinking back,

he poured himself
some coffee, sat
at the window,
watched the sparrows
searching in the woodpile
for the seed
he'd tossed them,
waited for the chickadees,
nuthatches, and juncos,
let the blue jays have their way.

Insomnia

Game plans swirl
in Coach's head
like a crowd
pushing for seats.
He imagines
Watts learning
to go to his left,
Thompson crashing
the boards, Donatelli
passing up a shot
to hit Wilson open
underneath. He grabs
his clipboard, diagrams
another way to spring
Kochinski free. He
walks to the window,
watches the snow falling
like losses settling along
the windowsill, goes
to the kitchen, pours
another cup of coffee,
stirs in some sugar.
It's four a.m. He thinks
of his wife, imagines
somewhere in her sleep
there floats a dream
that gets him out of last place.

Scrub

Last night at practice,
my man slipped by me
for a layup, and Coach
threw down his clipboard,
ran right up into my face,
slapped me behind the head,
and yelled, "What the hell
are you doing? Get in front.
Take a charge. You
on this team or not! How
are we gonna be ready if you
don't play tough defense?!"

Some mornings I wake up
wondering about tough defense,
and wind sprints, and running
up the bleachers twenty times.

Two hours every night
I'm on the other team.
I've heard it a thousand
times: "You're key to
this team. Without you
we'd never be ready." But
I know I do what you do
when you're never good enough.

Someday I'll come back
and point at that place on the bench.
Someday I'm gonna sit back,
watch TV, take a vacation

every summer, have a dog,
and never miss a game.

"You get in tonight?" my father asks
when I come in after the game.
I knock the snow from my boots.
"No." "Close game?" "No,
we lost by twenty-three." I
listen to the empty air, see
the slow shake of my father's
head, know he's been sitting
with a beer letting one sitcom
roll into the next, sneering at
the ads and laugh tracks, waiting
for the news, sports, and weather.
I go to the refrigerator, look at the line
of Budweiser cans, take out the milk,
pour a glass, go in with him
to watch the scores.

Sometimes, after practice,
I walk home slowly, and I
think about letting the ball
bounce away. Then I'd
sit down, let my mind
open up wider and wider,
so wide the sky would
come inside, the stars
would light it all.

Last week, after school,
my kid sister said, "I'm
scared the sun will go out."

"That's ridiculous. Can't
happen," and I took her hand,
looked out the window, up
into the sky, watched
the snow clouds cross.
"But it's fire," she said.
"Fire goes out."

Four wind sprints to go.
"Let's see what you have left.
Run. Run like I'm after you.
Run. Run now, or after the next
game, I'll run you till you drop.
Run, goddamn it, run."

Once last summer I lay in bed
wondering if somewhere hidden
in my cells was something good
enough that I could do. But
the cells were mute. The days
since then have been the same,
even their names dissolving
like the Host upon my tongue.

Coach Checks His Mail

Before heading to his classroom, he
goes to the office, pulls his mail
from the cubicle marked "Coach."
He remembers when the white tag
read "Mr. Daniels," how on the job's
first day, he paused over every
envelope, each flier, how he sorted
through everything, deciding
what to keep. He'd felt his nerves
were saying his name, that his life
was opening up wider than the hope
he slept in going through school.
Now he looks at ads for better socks,
a memo from the principal: "By
Tuesday, send the names of anyone
not passing to the office," a stack
of maps of Eastern Europe, and
an envelope with just his last name
scrawled across its front. He
opens it. His eyebrows tighten
at the dark, thick printing.
"Play my kid. If you don't, I'll
get the board to can your ass."
Coach stares at the name, sees
the kid behind each letter, puts
the note between the memo and
the maps, and heads to class.

Barber

Clipping around Coach's
ears, Barber says, "Hell,
I'm behind you, Coach,
no matter what. They talk
in here, you know. You
can imagine what they say.
I say we have to stand by
you. Tilt your head a bit.
It's a bad year. So what."

Coach hears the rumble
of a snowplow, watches
it go by hurling snow
high against the curb.
"Let me trim up the back
a bit. Then we'll be all set."

Coach stares into the mirror.
Barber taps his scissors
against his comb, shakes
the hair from the sheet.
"How's that look, Coach?"
"Looks good." Coach gets
up, pays. "You heading to
practice?" "Sure." Coach
puts on his coat. Barber
says, "With all this snow,
the crew will plow all night."
Coach nods, shoves his fingers
into his gloves. "Then I won't
have any trouble getting home."

Dog

Outside the gym,
in the parking lot,
during the game,
an old beagle
curled up under
a car. He'd wandered
down here toward
the lights, the noise,
through the snow,
his fur frozen, his
paws packed with ice.
Later, after the game,
as the crowd left,
they found him,
wondered where
he'd come from,
said, "Poor thing
must've crawled
under a car
to keep warm."
The next day,
Coach told his wife,
"After the game,
they found a dog
dead in the lot."

Coach Sits in Church Drawing a New Offense on the Front of the Sunday Bulletin

In two days, it'll be Wampton High,
14–2, and Coach hasn't got a clue
how he can penetrate their zone.
"Damn," he thinks, and scribbles
Xs and Os across the church's steeple.
"There's got to be a way."
His wife listens to the sermon.
Later, he'll ask her what it was
about. "The preacher said
learning to love is like teaching
the stones to talk." Coach shrugs.
"What do you make of that?" she
prods. "Hell, I don't know. I guess
he's right. Why make it harder than it is?"

He thinks, Jesus had it easy: forgave
everyone. Shut up the know-it-alls.
Turned water into wine. It took my mother
fourteen months to die. And I have to beat
these goddamned Tigers on my own.

Bus Driver

Standing at the back door, waiting
while the bus's engine hums
against the dark cold, its exhaust
a flume chilling into ice, melting
the snow beneath it, Driver, hands
in pockets, draws on his cigarette,
exhales, and feels the mean language
of age move in his bones.

Behind him, in the losers' locker room,
he knows his boys are dressing slowly,
staring into mirrors, setting their
wet hair straight, frowning at the way
they have to look, trying to think of
anything but the silent ride home.

The snow, packed hard now in midwinter,
squeaks under foot, and the air freezes
in the lungs, burns like a tongue
stuck to a frozen lamppost. Driver
glances at the bus, WILSON PUBLIC SCHOOLS
in black letters along its side, then up into
the sky, clouds crossing the full moon's
light like angels trying to comfort
anyone against a loss. The players

come out, pass him, step up into
the bus, find their seats. Coach
gets on last, sits in front. Driver
takes a last draw, feels the smoke
mix in his lungs, exhales, drops

the butt, a quiet hiss into the ice,
gets on and pulls the warm bus out,
across the empty lot, down a block,
left onto the highway home.

Scrub Dreams of Injuries

A twisted knee,
so he can limp
to class, feel
the delicate fingers
of the girl who didn't know
he loved her
gently touch the pain,
sending it into his heart.

A broken arm, slung
across his chest,
the cast a house
of itches he can't scratch,
a letter everyone can sign.

A cut lip, swollen,
the purple knot
so ugly, the girls
each want
to lay their lips
against it, soften
the flesh, let
the blood return
to its journey.

An ankle sprained so bad
it would be better broken.
He enters class on crutches,
lays them beside his desk;
enters the gym,
lays them beside the bench;
leaves on them after the game,
lays them beside his bed.

Coach's Prayer

Coach wonders if he prayed
would his luck change. God
could send a team of angels,
their snow white uniforms
without a wrinkle, halos perfect
rims above their sweet,
determined faces. Their wings
would wave, anxious to run
the infallible offense. Even
the benchwarmers would be
peaceful, their flawless hands
folded in their laps. The starting
five would grab the tip, dribble
through a sinful man-to-man,
and lift an alley-oop to any
open cherubim or seraphim
hovering above the hoop.
The other team would scream,
"Omniscience! Call them
for omniscience!" The refs
would shrug. Angels never
foul. They never watch the clock.
Coach would sit back, wait
until the final thirty seconds,
call time-out and gently tell them,
"Hold it for the final shot."

The Morning after the Tenth Straight Loss

"The only thing that's happy in my life,"
Coach thinks, "is my dog's tail." He looks
at his hands and wonders what they could
have held. It's a day when the temperature
will stay below zero. He goes upstairs,
all the losses lying in his mind's graveyard,
opens a window, reaches for the heat tape
dangling from the snow-covered roof, grabs it,
pulls it inside, plugs it in. His dog
has followed. Downstairs, on his bookshelf
are his gardening books: *The Gardener's
Garden, Guide to Creative Gardening, All
About Perennials.* In the fall, he strung
last summer's geraniums from a string
across the basement, the plants dangling
in the slant of light through the earth-high
windows. He goes back down, looks
at the morning paper, sees another
loss, goes to the shelf, takes *All About
Perennials,* goes to the living room, sits
on the sofa, one hand turning the pages,
one hand scratching his dog's right ear.

Team Meeting

"We stink," Coach growls,
staring at his players. They
feel every loss gather in
their necks. The weight of
silence settles like cement
in their shoes. "Would any
of you come watch us play?"
Their lips stiffen. "Ten in a
row. Ten! We even lost to
Jackson for Christ's sake.
We haven't lost to them in
ten years." He sighs, walks
slowly to the blackboard,
grabs a stick of chalk,
prints LOSERS across
the surface, draws a wide
circle around it, puts a star
above the circle. "I want
each of you to take this
chalk and write your name
inside that circle. Watts,
here, you start." Outside,
the snow is piling up
on cars and houses. Each
player writes his name. Coach
takes the chalk and adds his own.

Walking Home Late after Practice

Walking home late after practice,
Scrub kicks the snow, imagines

each flake a phony word, a lie,
a promise he believed, floating
up off into the air, mixing
in the wind, melting. Scrub

keeps walking, passes
under the streetlight across
from his house, sees the light on
in the kitchen, pauses, looks

back, suddenly starts to dance,
dance under the long deflected pass
of the moon's light. His feet
slide softly over the layers

of snow, piled and trampled hard
by schoolkids, teachers, people
heading to a friend's house. Scrub,
the dancer, whirling himself

into the soft night, into the wild
applause of the falling snow.

THE FOURTH QUARTER

Coach in Effigy

His daughter saw him first,
hanging from the maple
that draped its old arms
over the house, his head
blooming from the rope
that strangled his neck.
In the morning's moonlight,
she read their name
scrawled like a scar
across his chest. She
remembered the way
his hands had held her
years ago when, bloodied
from a fall, she'd let
the scream we carry
go to him. He seemed
to hold it in his hands.
Now, within this losing
season, she wants to take
this anonymous lynching
in her arms, ask the hands
that made it and the fists
that rose against it
to join, stand around her
as she sings the only song,
lets the head rest, lets
the heart give out.

Can't Sleep

Walking one night,
around two a.m.,
the snow drifting
in wide flakes
across the landscape

of lamplight, Coach
is struck by a gentle
fear that maybe
all he's given

up, all he's missed
is where he really lives:
Every word, note
of music, snowfall,

silly joke, something
as small as the dust
on a moth's wing, or as
large as the long, slow
look in a cow's eye, even

the quiet drift of every
evening, all wait
for him. Here
everything that has
no name is close as

breathing. He's walking
in a world without
a language, with no

thought to follow.
It's a world as strange
as the snowflake
melting on his hand.

Coach's Wife

She remembers
being happy,
looking forward
to something
besides another day
to get up,
make three meals
for a man who plays
golf and grows corn,
peas, beets, zucchini,
beans, tomatoes
that they can and store
in the basement
of the second house
they've built
here in the town
they've lived in
ever since they married
after college
when he took the job
as phys ed teacher,
backfield coach,
head man in basketball.
She remembers
her phone ringing,
walking late at night,
even dancing. Now
she leans on keeping
stats: logging lost
balls, rebounds, steals.

One Christmas she
gave the players
each a bow tie
she had made.

Coach Dreams of Being on Vacation

Swathed in Number 4 Coppertone,
Coach sits in his beach chair,
watching the Atlantic roll itself
toward his toes, his belly white
as a gull's, the sun playing him
tight. He listens to the waves,
the children squealing,
the stockbrokers still talking big bucks
as their wives try to coax them offshore,
and the teenagers laughing as they roll
under the cool water or whispering
as they bake next to each other, fingers
laced. Suddenly he wants to buy
some jeans, open his shirt, take
his wife across state lines.
But his brain's a gym.
Every move he makes draws jeers.
Even here, dreaming himself a surfer,
builder of sandcastles, a stud
who strolls the shoreline, or just
leaning back into the sand to feel
the salt air sift across his body,
he can hear the catcalls: "You're
a bum, Coach. You're a lousy bum."

The Next Morning

Driving to school,
after the latest
loss, Coach thinks
after the season's
over he will quit.
"I'll still teach."
He stares into his
rearview mirror
into the flutter
of snow. "I could
still coach—golf
or tennis, track."
The radio is on,
to the news. He
lets the good-
humored drone
of lost lives,
fires, robberies,
and presidential
updates pass across
him, then feels his
nerves draw tight,
they always do,
when the voice
says, "Wilson lost
again last night, 74
to 58. Today more
snow, high will be
17." Coach sees
his wife and his
daughter walking

against the eyes
that drop in front
of them. "Yeah,
maybe I'll quit."

Coach Teaching History

He's lied again.
He knows you never learn
a thing from any past.
His own history
is boredom, sullen kids,
and bills, this classroom
smell of too much perfume,
aftershave, and sweat.
He wants the past to be
a snowstorm keeping
him inside—just him,
his wife, an endless
night. They'd dance,
make love, and find
their bodies new again.
"History is hell,"
he says. The class
looks up. "Go find a job."

The Equipment Man's Wife

seldom goes to a game, is used
to dinner alone, keeping what's left
warm for when he gets home.
She loves to go to the movies, tunes
the radio to the oldies station
as she goes through her day. She
reads. When they were in high school,
they sat in the top row at every
home game, his arm draped over
her shoulder. "No PDA," their parents
told them. They didn't care. They
married a week after graduation. He
took a job at the tire store. They
raised two daughters, both now married,
kids of their own, living a day's
drive away. Two years with tires
was enough. He took the job
at the high school, picked up
the nickname Jeep. She thinks about
getting a new bedroom suite, some art
for the living room walls. Family
photographs hang above the fireplace,
sit on the mantel. She knows how
to make it through the winter
with her books, her knitting, her ways
of leafing through a magazine. Sometimes
they go for a drive on the weekend.
She likes to point out houses
she would love to live in.

Last Game

Heading to Sayersville,
Coach looks out the window
at the mud of early March
and says, "I want to be
cremated. Look at all that
land." Bus Driver nods,
says, "I'd like to buy
some land. Have a garden."
Coach says, "I don't want
to take up space." "You
think we'll beat these
guys tonight?" "Not a
chance." "Where you want
your ashes?" "Scattered."
"You want me to keep
a shot chart?" "Might
as well. Yeah, scatter 'em,
scatter 'em all over town."

Coach Reflects with His Wife
on the End of the Season

Couldn't we go
for a ride,
somewhere?
Couldn't we
start it all over,
find some way
to pass our time,
let it disappear.
You could sleep
quietly. I'd get
up early. We'd
sell antiques. We'd
open a little
restaurant, just
sandwiches and
delicious pies: apple,
blueberry, cherry,
pumpkin. In the fall,
we'd can vegetables.
We'd laugh as we
strained the plump,
red tomatoes. We'd
stare at the jars, let
their rich autumn
colors warm us
deep into winter.

On a Day in Early March

Coach needed more life insurance.
He hadn't thought about his plan
for years; then Bill Britson stopped
him on the street, confronted him
with the fact that his wife and
daughter wouldn't be left
with much unless he brought
his policies up to date. "We'll
look over the whole package, Coach,"
Bill said. "Can I stop by? This week?
How about Thursday, that be OK?"
Coach nodded. What did he know?
His kid could get along. His wife
could work. Besides, he'd never
die; his heart had pounded through
a dozen double overtimes, a thousand
snap decisions, all these losses, a life
of second guesses. But face it. Kids
were not the same and losses were
just losses now. And last night when
he looked in the mirror, he saw standing
there behind him, a high school forward,
ball on hip, hair slick and black, eyes
determined to stare down anyone stuck
with guarding him. He thought of
his letter sweater and the day he was
named the coach. Then he felt a hand
on his hip, an elbow heading toward his gut.

Late Night Jazz Station, Coach Listening

—for Paul Zimmer

Coach lets those good notes
float, swing their good way
into his late night. He smiles,
and his eyelids lower, and his
young dream comes sauntering
down the aisle of his mind.
He plays the sax.

Here, Coach, take it,
and he blows the meanest
wail, so mean that 'Trane
looks up, drops his chops,
Diz's cheeks collapse,
and Duke and Benny both turn
to Miles who laughs and says,
"Well, Count, we've all been had."

Coach is hot. The whole joint
is swinging as he leans down,
blowing his whole damn life out
his horn. Everyone's clapping,
stomping, screaming, "Yeah!"

Even Bird is flattened, floored,
turns to Mingus, says, "That's
it. We got a sax." Coach
can't believe his ears. He hits
one more long and loving note,
letting it hang in the air, feeling

the reed go limp against his tongue.
No one says a word.

Coach looks up,
gives them all a nod,
and takes his leave, the
whole place wondering
where the hell he's been
and where the hell he's going.

All He Does

"He's still playing ball," Star's mother
says to his father, both of them
standing over the kitchen sink,
looking out at their son as he whirls,
dribbles with his left hand, crosses
to the top of the key he and his father
painted on the driveway when Star
was seven. Now seventeen, he was
hot for twenty-six a game throughout
the losing season. Every spring
they repaint the key. "He can't
play ball forever," she says. "He
can go to college," he says. "He'll
get a damn good job." She hands him
a wet plate. He rubs the towel across it,
says, "His grades are good enough.
He'll get a scholarship. He will."
They watch him grab his own missed shot,
take the ball back out beyond the circle,
dribble through his legs, fake left, drive
right, stop, jump, hit, and pump his fist.
He works the corners, moves around the key,
gives a sudden fake, a swift shimmy
of his shoulders, then lifts his jump shot
soft into the air, his breathing calm as sleep.

Dear Coach

Dear Coach,

Remember the time you left me in after I'd missed seven in a row, tossed a few out of bounds, and let my man score twenty? Bad night. But you didn't pull me. You must have taken a lot for that. I can still hear the boos. I thought they were all at me. Why'd you leave me in? I've thought about that lately. Did you really think I'd come around? The other guys were furious sitting there watching me screw up. And after the game? What did you say? You must have had a second thought. It hit me last week. I was thinking back, remembering certain games. After that one, I wanted to run away. I had a thousand excuses. My family's fine, kids are growing up. We took a vacation this year. My mother's doing OK. Business is business, up and down. If you're ever in town, I sure hope you'll stop to see us.

Best ——

Coach Tells His Wife about the Big Game, the Big Snow

"We'd won thirty-seven straight here! I played guard. One time, it was in January, we were behind by fifteen with four minutes to go—and won by five. The game ended on a hook by Tom Branch from mid-court, cut the nets with the goddamned thing. During the second half the snow started falling. By the time we stopped chanting, 'We're number one!' the stuff had piled up over I'd say twenty inches. Every car, all the buses, were buried. That same night Bob's dog got lost. That dog had slept in nearly every house in town. No one ever found it, not even in March. And the cars, we had no idea what to do about them. A few guys went home and got shovels. But there was too much snow and there were too many cars. I don't know who threw the first snowball. But one was enough. When the team came out, they belted us. And we started throwing at them. And then everyone started firing at everyone. They did get the buses out. But most of the cars were there all night. I remember ducking behind Ken Lacey's Buick. Somebody lobbed a couple balls over the car, and I dodged them. Then I just sat down in the stuff. The sky by now was clear, and it seemed that someone had tossed every snowball in the world up into that roof, where each one stuck and stayed. I felt right then I could call it quits. You ask anyone about that night; they'll all say something happened there. The next morning, that was exactly what my father said: 'Something happened there,' and then he told us to shape up in school and kissed us and went to work, and I imagined he was happy. Of course, there was no school. We made a good bit of money shoveling. By afternoon, all the cars were out. Even now, on certain nights when I look at the sky, I see all those snowballs. Hell, they won't ever melt."

Night Gym

The gym is closed, locked
for the night. Through
the windows, a quiet
beam from the streetlights
lies across center court.
The darkness wraps itself
around the trophies, lies
softly on Coach's desk,
settles in the corners.
A few mice scratch under
the stands and at the door
of the concession booth.
The night wind rattles
the glass in the front doors.
The furnace, reliable
as grace, sends its steady
warmth through the rafters,
under the bleachers, down
the halls, into the offices
and locker rooms. Outside,
the snow falls, swirls, piles
up against the entrance.

ACKNOWLEDGMENTS

Grateful acknowledgment is made to the editors of the following maga-
zines in which many of these poems first appeared, sometimes in different
versions: *Aethlon, Artful Dodge, Carolina Quarterly, The Chaminade Literary
Review, The Chariton Review, Chelsea, Dirty Goat, Elkhorn Review, 5 A.M.,
Free Lunch, The Listening Eye, Nebraska Territory, The New York Quarterly,
Passages North, Ploughshares, Poetry East, Samisdat, Sandscript, SKY,
Tamaqua, The Westminster Review, Wind, Windless Orchard,* and *Yarrow.*

Grateful acknowledgment is also made to the editors and publishers of the
following anthologies in which some of these poems have appeared: *For
a Living,* edited by Peter Oresick and Nicholas Coles (University of Illinois
Press, 1995); *Full Court,* edited by Dennis Trudell (Breakaway Books, 1996);
Looking for Your Name, edited by Paul B. Janeczko (Orchard Books, 1993);
Men of Our Time, edited by Fred Moramarco and Al Zolynas (University of
Georgia Press, 1992); *New Poems from the Third Coast,* edited by Michael
Delp, Conrad Hilberry, and Josie Kearns (Wayne State University Press,
2000).

Some of these poems have also appeared in the chapbook *After School*
(Samisdat Press, 1988); and in *between* (Dawn Valley Press, 1988).

Special thanks to Myra Kohsel and Julie Ridl for their hours of patient help
in preparing the manuscript and to all those who have helped these poems
and believed in this collection and supported this poet over the years. I'm
afraid I'll leave someone out, so I hope you know who you are and how
grateful I am.

OTHER BOOKS IN THE NOTABLE VOICES SERIES

CAVANKERRY'S MISSION

Through publishing and programming, CavanKerry Press connects communities of writers with communities of readers. We publish poetry that reaches from the page to include the reader, by the finest new and established contemporary writers. Our programming brings our books and our poets to people where they live, cultivating new audiences and nourishing established ones.

CavanKerry now uses only recycled paper in its book production. Printing this book on 30% PCW and FSC certified paper saved 2 trees, 1 million BTUs of energy, 127 lbs. of CO_2, 67 lbs. of solid waste, and 524 gallons of water.